PROFE____IO___
TABLE TENNIS
COACHES
HANDBOOK

©2013 By Larry Hodges
USATT Certified National Coach & Hall of Famer
www.TableTennisCoaching.com

Cover photo by Mike Yuan

Version April 8, 2013

Table of Contents

Foreword

If you are reading this you are probably either a professional table tennis coach or are thinking of becoming one. This manual should help in either case.

This manual is not about coaching technique, but how to set up and run a coaching business – the finances, getting a facility and equipment, setting up and running coaching programs, and (most important) getting and keeping students, which is the bloodline of your coaching business. This is all about how to make a living as a *Professional Table Tennis Coach*. However, the info in this handbook should be useful to anyone who is actively coaching.

For info on coaching techniques, see USATT's *Instructor's Guide to Table Tennis* (a basics manual I wrote), the ITTF's coaching manuals, or any of a number of books and videos that teach playing and coaching techniques. (See chapter on Helpful Links and Resources.) If you have knowledge of the game as a player, you'll learn the rest with training and experience. You should also attend a coaching clinic for coaches (USATT runs several each year), or attend a coaching camp as an assistant to observe professional coaches at work.

It is assumed that the reader is fairly experienced as a player. To be a coach, you do not need to be a top player, although it helps. You do not need to have extensive coaching experience – no one does when they begin. You simply have a desire to be a coach in the Olympic Sport of Table Tennis.

For information on becoming a
USATT or ITTF Certified Coach,
go to www.usatt.org.
This is strongly recommended!

USA
TABLE TENNIS

CHAPTER ONE
The Profession of Coaching

There are two types of professional coaches: part-time coaches, and full-time coaches whose primary income is from coaching (or related income). If you are thinking of becoming a full-time coach, with table tennis your primary income, you need to ask yourself the following questions:

- Do you like coaching? (If not, go no farther.)
- Will the income be adequate for your needs? (See next chapter.)
- Is your table tennis level and knowledge high enough so that you can work with players at the beginning/intermediate level?
- Are you physically able to coach the amount of hours needed? (Group coaching is less demanding, but it's sometimes difficult to get enough students from that alone.)
- Are you determined to become the best coach you possibly can? (Anything less is unfair to yourself and your students.)

If your answers to the above questions is no, then you might not want to be a full-time coach. But if you say yes to all of them, then you are about to enter the corps of Professional Table Tennis Coaches. Welcome!

Teaching the forepaw to your students. Photo by Mal Anderson

CHAPTER TWO
How Much Income Can You Make as a Table Tennis Coach?

Can you make a living at table tennis? Let's look at potential income from private coaching alone.

Annual Salary, 50 Weeks/Year, Private Coaching Only

Hours/week	$25/hour	$30/hour	$35/hour	$40/hour	$45/hour	$50/hour
5	$ 6,250	$ 7,500	$ 8,750	$10,000	$11,250	$12,500
10	$12,500	$15,000	$17,500	$20,000	$22,500	$25,000
15	$18,750	$22,500	$26,250	$30,000	$33,750	$37,500
20	$25,000	$30,000	$35,000	$40,000	$45,000	$50,000
25	$31,250	$37,500	$43,750	$50,000	$56,250	$62,500
30	$37,500	$45,000	$52,500	$60,000	$67,500	$75,000
35	$43,750	$52,500	$61,250	$70,000	$78,750	$87,500
40	$50,000	$60,000	$70,000	$80,000	$90,000	$100,000

Are these figures reasonable? There are numerous coaches in the U.S. who coach 40-50 hours or more a week at $40-$50/hour, plus group sessions, and make over $200,000/year coaching. Any coach who lives near a reasonably large population base can within 2-3 months get about as many hours of coaching as he/she wishes. It can get physically exhausting, especially when you do private coaching for 25-30 hours per week or more, so you might want to set an upper limit for private coaching, and then add as many group sessions as possible.

But this doesn't realistically show how much money one can make at table tennis – you can (and should!) make more. Here are a few examples.

Income from a Junior Training Program
Suppose you have 20 junior players paying $15 per 2-hour session, twice per week. (More later on how to get students.) That's $600/week for four hours work, or $150/hour! Do that for 50 weeks, and you're making $30,000/year from this alone. You might want an assistant coach or practice partners, and you may have to pay a percentage to the club or facility, but you should still get the bulk of this income. Plus it'll be a main source for private students. (Some professional coaches rely mostly on group sessions, and do little private coaching.)

Income from a Beginning Class

Suppose you set up a 10-week, 90-minute/session beginning class. Suppose you get 20 players at $120 each, and hire one assistant coach (often a local player) at $20/hour, or $30/session. That's $2400 in income. After you pay $300 for the assistant coach, you come out with a $2100 profit for 15 hours of work. That's $140/hour! (Again, some of this might go to your club.)

Suppose you do four classes like this per year: add about $8400 to your annual income. (Not to mention the extra money from private students you get from the class, sales of equipment and refreshments, club fees if they join your club, tournament and/or league fees if you run them, etc.) Or you could even do just the class, and pocket the $8400/year. The players get what they paid for (if you are a good coach); the local club, tournaments, and leagues get new players, and you get a nice salary for your work. *Everybody wins!*

Income from Tournaments

Suppose, in addition to coaching, you run tournaments and leagues. Besides giving students more incentive to improve (and thus seek out the local professional coach – you), you will get income from these tournaments and leagues. The actual running of these events is outside the scope of this manual (contact USATT for more info on this), but they are related to coaching. If you don't run these types of programs, make sure someone else does so, for the benefit of your students – and yourself, since your students will be more active and more likely to continue if they have programs like these.

Suppose you decide to run a tournament every two months. Suppose you get 60 players each time, at $50/each, $3000 income. Suppose you give out $1000 in prize money and trophies, and an additional $500 in expenses – mailings, flyers, hired staff, sanction fee, etc. That's a profit of $1500 for one or two day's work ($9,000/year) – plus profits from sales of refreshments and equipment. In addition, you can often set up mini-clinics on the Friday before a tournament for extra income.

Income from Leagues

Suppose you run a weekly league and get 20 players at $7/night each. That's $140 for each league night, or about $7000/year.

Income from Equipment and Refreshment Sales

Contact various table tennis companies about being an equipment distributor. Your students will need equipment, and they'll either buy it from you – or from someone else. Why not you? Similarly, if you have refreshments on hand (especially drinks), you'll make profits from that.

Payments to Your Club

Unless you actually own your own club or coach at a free facility, you may have to pay something to the club in return for coaching. However, nearly all successful clubs learn that if they try to "tax" the coaches too much, the coaches lose incentive, and both sides lose. Instead, stress to club owners that if they keep payments by coaches to the club minimal, the coaches will bring in lots of students who will bring money to the club directly with memberships, tournament fees, league fees, equipment sales, refreshments, as well as a percentage of group and private coaching fees. A good arrangement for a full-time coach is to pay the club $10/hour for the first 20 hours of private coaching each week, with no charge for the rest. For group sessions, which take up more tables but bring in more revenue, $20/hour is a reasonable arrangement. Or perhaps, if you coach full-time, just pay the club a set monthly fee, such as $500/month.

Coaches that pay a lot to the club tend to coach less and soon go to another club or leave the coaching profession. Clubs that rely directly on coaches to pay for a substantial portion of their expenses end up with coaches that don't work as much or who leave, and who don't bring in players. Coaches should make good money for their work. If the coach does well, so does the club. A club that's full of players that the coach brought in is a successful club that's going to make plenty of income from all these players.

Total Income

You should be able to make $60,000/year in 25 hours coaching per week (including some group sessions), and more if you get income from tournaments, leagues, and equipment & refreshment sales.

CHAPTER THREE
What Credentials Do You Need to Be a
Table Tennis Coach?

Not as much as you'd think. Let's start with playing level.

What Level Player Does a Professional Table Tennis Coach Need To Be?

Let's be real. To be a professional table tennis coach, you need to be (or have been) at a certain level as a player. Being able to play an orthodox game with orthodox strokes is also important – if you can't demonstrate it, how can you teach it effectively? Using the USATT rating system, anybody over an 1800 level would have no trouble making it as a coach. There are a number of success stories of coaches at that level or even lower. If your goal is to coach mostly beginners, then you don't need a high level of play; you only need a high level of knowledge. As your aspirations go higher, your level of play may become more important.

Remember – to a typical beginning player, an 1800 player looks like the world champion. You may be hesitant about your knowledge and abilities as a coach, but as an experienced player, you know so much more than beginners that you'll be coaching them for months before you run out of things to teach – and by then, you'll be on your way toward being an experienced coach.

You'll find that getting credentials is not as difficult as you'd think. There are two types of credentials that are helpful for coaches: playing credentials and coaching credentials. Almost any current or past title can help you as a player – county champion, local collegiate champion, etc. If you have anything like this, it'll help in getting students. As to coaching credentials, at the very least, get certified as a coach by USATT or ITTF. (USATT is moving toward using the ITTF certification process, so soon they may be the same thing.)

USATT and ITTF Coaching Certification

For info on being certified as a USATT Coach, see the USA Table Tennis web page at www.usatt.org. If you are experienced as a player, you will not have too much difficulty in getting certified at least at the club level. (The coaching levels are Club, State, Regional and National.) As you gain experience, you can move up the ladder to

National Coach. By being certified, you will be listed as a coach on the USATT coaches list, with contact info. As a USA Table Tennis Certified Coach, you will receive information on coaching seminars and other materials so you can expand your table tennis knowledge. (Contact USA Table Tennis for information on this.) Plus, getting certified gives you a nice USATT Certified Coach Certificate for the wall at your club!

Note that USATT is moving toward adopting the ITTF certification process, and that if you are ITTF certified, you automatically become USATT certified.

Credentials or not, what do you need to know to be a professional table tennis coach? Obviously, you need to know the techniques that you will be teaching. If you are an experienced player, you'll know the basics – but will need to know some of the specifics of the techniques (i.e. you may be doing something correctly, but not really know what you are doing), and you'll need to know how to teach it. However, if you are an experienced player, you know all you need to start out as a coach, as long as you actively expand your coaching skills.

Certified Umpire

You may also find it valuable to get certified as an umpire. It's often surprising how many coaches aren't well versed in the rules. It's a simple test (at the lowest levels), and is something all coaches should do. And it's another certificate for your wall! Info on this is at www.usatt.org.

CHAPTER FOUR
Getting a Facility, Tables, and Other Equipment

If there isn't already a facility with tables for you to coach at, then you're going to have to do some legwork to get them. If you want to be a full-time coach, then you'll need either a full-time facility, or several locations to coach at.

For many coaches, there may already be a local club, but it's only part-time – and the tables are used by club members. This doesn't leave you with tables to coach on. For part-time coaching, you might ask the club leaders if you can use one table to coach on, in return for either a percentage of coaching, or for promoting the club or other work. Typically, a club should let you coach for free at the start. After you've built up your business, you should pay the club either a percentage of your coaching income (perhaps for the first 20 hours per week only) or a set monthly fee, perhaps $500/month if you are coaching full time. Not only does the coach get income this way, but you attract new players for them – so make sure to point this out to them when bargaining on the finances!

If you are looking for a new facility to coach at, there are many options. Get out the phone book and start out by contacting local recreation centers. (They may be listed under "community centers.") Local schools and churches are also possibilities – for these, you might ask local players about possibilities.

Schools can be a great resource. A survey done by this author a number of years ago showed that about 1/3 of junior and high schools already have ping pong tables, and many of those schools already have ping pong clubs. Find all the schools in your area with tables and clubs, and get in contact with them about coaching or using their facilities.

Full-Time Clubs
Circa 2006, there were only about ten full-time professional clubs in the USA. Since that time there's been an explosion, and as of April, 2013, there were nearly 60 of them. If you want to be a full-time professional coach, the best thing you can do is either find a full-time facility you can coach at, or start one up yourself.

Tables, Nets, Barriers, Balls and Robots

You need to supply the tables, nets, barriers, and balls for training.

If you're not rich, contact table tennis distributors about getting discounts on these items. One way to get a good deal is to agree to sell only equipment from the manufacturer/distributor that gives or discounts the equipment for you. Most are willing to make deals if you become a distributor for them. You'll need a lot of balls for your coaching (especially multiball). You'll also want a number of low-end rackets for beginners.

After the U.S. Open, U.S. Nationals and North American Teams (and often other large tournaments), the used tables, nets and barriers are normally on sale at a discount, and the distributors will allow you to pay for them monthly (installment plan), with interest based on your credit rating. Contact the tournament directors or table dealer for further info. If you combine this with becoming a distributor for the table manufacturer's equipment, you might get a very good deal. Another option is to contact local clubs to see if they have used tables for sale. Many clubs are willing to sell older tables, and use the money to help pay for new ones.

Balls are an ongoing expense. As a coach, you will go through a lot of them due to multi-ball training and group training. Most full-time coaches work out some sort of deal with a distributor for free or inexpensive training balls. (You can also get deals for 3-star balls for tournaments.) You'll also want ball pick-up nets so you and students don't spend half their time picking up balls during sessions. Some prefer the ball pick-up tubes.

College Classes

Most colleges have numerous sports classes, and welcome the idea of a table tennis class. Contact the local colleges' physical education departments, and ask about setting one up. You'll find that most colleges already have tables – so that problem is taken care of. Even if you coach at a club, this is a great way of getting new players into your club.

Table Tennis Robots

Robots are valuable tools for coaches, and I recommend you get one. They are very good for beginners to work on basic strokes. They are also useful for group training when you have an odd number of players. They are also a great attraction for junior players, who love to use them. Like other equipment items, you can become a robot dealer, and in return get a deal on it for your coaching.

There are really nice ones on the market now that can do all sorts of drills. However, they are rather expensive. You might have to go with the cheaper models that only hit to one spot, unless you have it oscillate back and forth, leading to a random spray of balls, which isn't usually too helpful. I've used the lower-end ones pretty much exclusively for many years, as they are pretty good practice for beginners.

Using Videotape

One way to both increase interest AND improve your coaching is to make use of videotape. If you have a video camera, you may charge a nominal fee for a tape of your sessions. Then, when giving lessons, refer to what the player can now see in the tapes. See links to online videos in the Links & Resources section.

CHAPTER FIVE
Start With a Plan

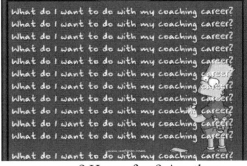

No two regions have exactly the same circumstances, so you need to tailor your coaching program to your circumstances and personal preferences. How many tables can you use? How often? Are there already established players looking for coaching, or are you starting from scratch? Do you prefer coaching adults, juniors, beginners or advanced players? (Can you afford to be choosy?)

You need to decide what your goals as a coach are. If it's simply to make lots of money, and that alone, you are probably in the wrong profession. (Though you can make pretty good money coaching!) If it's because you enjoy coaching, and want to make a living at it – then you're in business. But you need to be more specific.

Some coaches are picky about their students, and only want to coach players who can become elite players. If you can afford to pick and choose your students, you can do that. If you are trying to make a living, or at least make good money at it, you can't afford to be too choosy – at least at the start. As you pick up business, you might be able to pick and choose.

Questions to ask yourself:
- Do you prefer to do group training or private coaching?
- How serious should the training be? Every coach has to find a balance between seriousness and fun.
- How many hours a week can you coach?
- How many hours a week do you need to coach to make the amount of money you need to make?

Here are some coaching options to choose from:
- Private Coaching
- Beginning Classes
- Intermediate/Advanced Classes
- Junior Training Classes

Multi-ball Training

You also have to choose how you will coach. Will you mostly hit with your private students, one on one? In group sessions, will you mostly coach by walking around as students hit with each other? Or will you use multi-ball training as well? I strongly recommend

Multi-ball training

incorporating multi-ball every chance you can, and become an expert at it. You'll need a box of balls. Standing at the side of the table (though some will sometimes do this from the end of the table), simply hit the balls at the player at whatever speed, pace, direction, depth, and spin is needed for a given drill. You can do pattern drills as well. If possible, get a net for the end of the table (such as the ones used in table tennis robots), though picking up the balls is a good break for the player.

CHAPTER SIX
Recruiting Students
Recruiting students, along with coaching well, are the most important tasks for any coach!

You'll need to create a flyer about your coaching program. It should include your name, any titles as a player or coach, contact info, rates and hours, and what type of coaching you do (private, group, what type of classes, etc.). You should also create a web page, which you can refer to when you promote your coaching. It could be your own web page, or a page at your club's web page.

Ways to publicize your coaching and recruit students
It's important that you do all of these!
1. Email copies of your coaching flyer and press release to the calendar section of every newspaper in town.
2. Give copies of the flyer to all local club members to give out to interested parties. Family members of current club members are a treasure trove of potential students.
3. Do a mailing to all current and past USATT members in your region. You can get address labels cheaply from USATT. You can get them by age, by zip code, or just about anything else.
4. Put up copies on every bulletin board you can find, including recreation centers, YMCA's, Boys' Clubs and colleges. It might be a good idea to create a flyer with tear-off phone numbers at the bottom. You may have to get permission first.
5. Distribute the flyer at Asian Restaurants and Churches. Look them up in the phone book, and mail, fax, or email the flyer.
6. Contact local Chinese schools. You can find these either in the yellow pages, or simply ask local Chinese players. Most Chinese schools meet in regular schools, but on weekends. This is a treasure trove for students.
7. Contact local schools and offer to do exhibitions or to teach a PE class. Bring lots of flyers to give out. (Get permission first.) You might consider a free introductory class for juniors, perhaps six weeks long, once per week, as a "hook" to bring in new players. Or a free 30-minute lesson to new juniors.
8. Contact local newspapers & TV about doing stories on local table tennis.
9. Advertise on craigslist.com and other Internet sites.
10. Put flyers in bottles and toss them out to sea.

Let's elaborate on item #1, one of the most important. This is what you are going to do.

1. Pick up Yellow Pages, or do an Internet search, and find every local newspaper. Make a list of their phone numbers
2. Call every local newspaper, and ask for the email address for the calendar section of their newspaper.
3. Send a press release and copy of your flyer to every newspaper in town. Or look at sample calendar sections, and send them something that fits their format.
4. Make sure to send notice of your classes at least six weeks before the start of every new beginning class.
5. Enjoy the free advertising! And it's perfect for a table tennis class as the people who look at newspaper calendar sections are usually those looking for a new activity.

See the sample press release and flyers in Sample Flyers chapter at end.

Recruiting Junior Players

Recruiting junior players (from around ages 7 to 17) has always been a difficult task, but usually because it is done in such a haphazard fashion. The three most important things in recruiting juniors are:

1. **Have a program.** New junior players will rarely join a club if they have to call winners on a table against an older player who beats them badly, and where most club members avoid them because they are beginners.
2. **Promote the program.** No one will come to your program if they don't know about it. Recruit it with every method at your disposal.
3. **Have other juniors.** Junior players want to be in programs with other players their age. This is the single most important concept in setting up a junior program.

To those setting up a program from scratch, item #3 seems contradictory – to get juniors, you need juniors. *Where do you begin???*

The key thing is to set up a training program and then promote it so that you reach "critical mass" – enough junior players that the program is attractive to new juniors. At that point, the program becomes nearly self-supporting, with players joining in as fast or faster than they leave, and you are forced to have a waiting list. A successful junior program may not need to actively recruit new players – once they reach this critical mass, it becomes self-supporting through word of mouth – and your goal should be to reach this stage. How do you do this?

Over and over junior programs fail because a coach is determined to build it up until it is a success. What they don't know is that they probably have already failed. It may sound good, but trying to build up a junior program gradually means you'll be losing players as fast as you get them, leading to a constant struggle to fill the sessions up.

The key is to have a large number of juniors **on the first day.** This means using all of the methods at your disposal to make certain that there are at least 12-15 juniors at the first session. See the list above of ways to recruit students. Set a date for the first session, and **use all of these methods** at the same time to make sure to fill the class up on the first day.

Another way to fill up a junior class, as well as to bring in practice partners for beginning juniors, is to offer the sessions for free for a period of time to more advanced juniors, in return for their hitting with beginning players a portion of each session.

CHAPTER SEVEN
Setting Up and Teaching a Class

This is a must for successful coaches, so let's go over it step by step. You might have to make adjustments for your particular program. For example, if you are teaching a college class, you might have to adjust to the college's schedule, or their academic requirements. Beginning classes are important for bringing in new players and are highly popular, but you can and should also have intermediate and advanced training for ongoing players. Junior classes are different, and are covered in the next chapter.

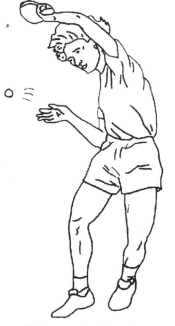

Step One: Should You Hire an Assistant Coach?

You may need an assistant coach or practice partners, depending on the number of players in the class. (You need to decide how many players you can have as a maximum, and stick to that. If you get too many, set up a second class.) The assistant coach need not be a regular coach – just a reasonably good player. The assistant coach gets paid for his work, which comes out of the class fees, perhaps $15-20/hour. It's easy to get volunteers to do the class for a time, but unless they get paid, their interest goes down, and eventually you lose them. If you get a lot of students, there's a lot of cash coming in, and they will enjoy it far more if you have an assistant coach or practice partners. In the long wrong, via repeat customers and word of mouth, you'll come out ahead. Most importantly, you and the students will enjoy it more.

Step Two: Create a Schedule

For a beginning class, I recommend roughly 7-8:30pm or 7:30-9:00pm once a week for ten weeks. Many clubs get busy around 8pm; if so, perhaps make it 6:30-8:00pm. On weekends, you can move it around some to fit your schedule.

Step Three: Produce a Flyer

You will need to produce an info flyer, and make lots of copies of it. (See sample flyers at the end of this handbook.) The flyer should specify that the class is for beginners or those who have not been in organized table tennis, or whatever the criteria is for the class. The flyer should include the following information:

- The names of the coaches and their qualifications.
- The address & directions to site.
- Contact information for further information.
- The fee and who/what to make it out to. $100 for a ten-week, 15-hour class seems reasonable, though some might charge more. I recommend keeping prices down - the priority is to fill the class and get them into the sport for the long term.
- Dates and times of the class.
- If it's not strictly a Beginning Class, then an approximate rating level the class is for, for the benefit of USTTA-rated players (under 1300, for example).
- A short listing of the things to be covered in the class.

Step Four: Develop a Class Plan

What follows is a sample schedule for a ten-week, 90 minutes/week Beginning Class, used for years in Maryland. Feel free to make your own adjustments.

Week 1:	Intro to TT; Grip; Stance; Forehand drive
Week 2:	Table tennis equipment; Backhand drive
Week 3:	Footwork; Beginning serves
Week 4:	Pushing; Advanced serves
Week 5:	FH loop vs. backspin; Blocking
Week 6:	BH attack
Week 7:	Smashing
Week 8:	Return of Serve
Week 9:	Loop/smash combinations; Tactics
Week 10:	Smashing lobs; Player's choice; 11-point games

You might want to schedule a USATT tournament at the end or near the end of the class, with a novice singles event for class participants.

Step Five:
Collect fees, and teach the class! Make sure to get contact information for everyone so you can send them info on future programs.

Step Six:
See Step One. Every time it gets easier!

Teaching the Beginning Class
Start off each session with some easy stretching. Next, ask if there are any questions from the previous week. Next, explain & demonstrate the first item planned for that week's class. Finally, send the players to the tables (one group per coach, if you have multiple coaches) to work on the technique. If two items are scheduled for that day, make sure to plan how long to spend on each segment. When the first segment is done, call everyone together again, and explain & demonstrate the next technique.

Don't get too caught up with the idea of trying to make everyone a world-class player. Most are there not only to learn, but to have fun as well. Keep that in mind as you teach.

Some of the players will develop nice strokes, while others will have rather strange ones. If a player is resistant to change, work with him, and make the best of what he does.

There are three methods of practice you should use in teaching the class. The most important is multi-ball. If you have assistant coach or practice partners, break the class into groups with each coach feeding multi-ball. Have the players rotate – one gets multi-ball, one or two pick up balls, and the rest either rest or practice on separate tables. Multi-ball is especially good when teaching a new stroke.

A second method is to have the coaches/helpers hit with each of the players. This is especially good when teaching them stroking and footwork drills.

A third method is to have the players practice together. This is the easiest way, but is the least effective as the players, at this level, simply can't rally effectively or consistently. They will learn much faster if they sometimes hit with an accomplished player who can adjust for their errors and keep the ball going at the same pace, same spot. Pushing is a good stroke to have the players hit among themselves, although the coaches/helpers should step in and hit with those who are having difficulty. Serve and receive practice can also be done among the players, with one player serving and catching the other's receive, or both players serving and catching the other's serve. Or, if you have enough balls and tables, let the players serve onto the floor and pick them up afterwards.

Reminder – make sure to get contact information for everyone so you can send them info on future programs.

Intermediate and Advanced Training
These are a lot easier to run. Unlike beginners, intermediate and advanced players can already do the basic shot, and so you can put them on the tables (pairing them roughly by level), and call out the drills. Instead of focusing on teaching the basics, you can now do more individual work with each player. Here's a sample session for a typical 90-minute session, which I find a good length for adults, who follow this up with open play on their own. See Drills Library to choose appropriate drills.

1. Jogging & Stretching – 5 minutes
2. Forehand & backhand warm-up (drives & loops) – 10 minutes
3. Footwork/Stroking Drill #1 – 15 minutes
4. Footwork/Stroking Drill #2 – 15 minutes
5. Break – 5 minutes
6. Footwork/Stroking Drill #3 – 15 minutes
   (This could also be a serve or receive drill)
7. Drill #4 (serve & attack drill) – 15 minutes
8. Serve practice – 10 minutes
   (You could replace this with 10 minutes of counterlooping or a
similar drill, and move it earlier in the session.)

CHAPTER EIGHT
Setting Up and Running a Junior Training Program

Why a Junior Training Program?

Some would say that if you have to ask, there's no point in explaining. Why is there Little League Baseball? Nearly every other sport in the U.S. has junior programs, whether it be baseball, basketball, football, soccer, tennis, softball, lacrosse, etc. Why not table tennis?

There's another reason to set up a junior program – you get paid for it. See the chapter on "How Much Income Can You Make as a Table Tennis Coach?" Plus, if you are a full-time coach – or hope to become one – this is where you get your students from.

There are two parts to setting up and running a junior training program. First, you have to know how to set it up, which includes recruiting the players. That is covered in the chapter on "Recruiting Students." The key thing about recruiting juniors is that cannot grow it slowly, or you'll lose junior players as fast as you get them. You need a large core of players on day one, at least 12-15. Fewer than that, and the lack of players, and divergence in ages and levels, make it less interesting to the kids. So you must use all the methods outlined in the junior section on "Recruiting Students" **at the same time**, and maximize how many show up on Day One of your junior program.

Second, you have to know how to teach it – specifically, how to coach juniors, as opposed to coaching adults. That is what is covered in this chapter.

How It's Different

Coaching junior players is somewhat different than coaching adults. In terms of teaching, juniors tend to pick up new techniques faster and better, but don't have the ball control that will develop as they get older and develop better motor skills.

They also don't have the attention span of adults. With an adult, you may spend a lot of time on one thing, trying to get it right. Except for advanced juniors (with a larger investment in the sport), this won't work as well with junior players. This doesn't mean breezing through something and not teaching it well. It means that while an adult may spend a long time working on something new, a junior player probably would spend less time in one session on the same technique. Otherwise, the junior will simply lose interest and look to other activities. Generally, I wouldn't have most beginning/intermediate juniors spend more than half an hour on one technique – it's not worth the risk of "burn-out." (However, for beginners, where everything is new and exciting, you can sometimes have them work on one stroke for longer periods of time.)

Discipline

One of the toughest tasks a new coach faces when working with junior players for the first time in a group session is discipline. Many coaches know a lot about table tennis, but not how to motivate and keep discipline. It doesn't take long to lose control of a class, and once lost, discipline is hard to regain.

Start off by deciding exactly what you think you should fairly expect from the players. If it's a two-hour session, do you expect them to focus continuously on training the entire time? Unless you've got a room full of advanced junior players (i.e., more used to the discipline needed to improve), you're kidding yourself if you do. You've got find a balance between work and play. If the juniors know that the first half will be training, the second half more games, they are more willing to concentrate for the first half, knowing the second half will be more "fun." Yet, even the fun part is training, since they will be playing competitive matches. So a good balance would be to let the players know that the first half will be all training; the second half might start with a drill or two, but then go into match play or games of some sort.

What do you do if the players goof off during the training part? Let it be known that the harder they work the first half, the sooner they will get to the game part in the second half. Then stick to it. (Never threaten a disciplinary action you are not prepared to fulfill.) You'll be surprised at how this gets them to focus!

If a player really is causing a problem, have him to sit out for a while. Few players want to sit on the sidelines while the rest are playing or practicing.

What To Do With Beginning Players?

The problem is that beginners, especially younger juniors, can't really rally properly together, and so putting them together too much doesn't help. You can put them with an assistant coach for a portion of a session, but there is a limit to how much attention one player can get. One option is to put them with a robot, which can help them develop the basics. However, ideally you want them to hit with real people. There are really two options.

When you begin your junior program and have a group of new juniors, recruit local players and juniors to help out temporarily. You may be surprised at the positive response. Try and get a number of players who can help out as coaches. Instead of live play, have them feed multi-ball to the new juniors, with 2-4 kids per table. After a dozen sessions, the kids will be ready to hit among themselves.

You should also offer free sessions to more advanced juniors if they will spend an hour each session with a beginning junior. This will further speed up their development. It also brings in more local juniors, making the entire program more favorable to new juniors.

If you absolutely cannot bring in additional coaches on a temporary basis, you could require new juniors to take a few hours of private coaching before being allowed in the class. If you absolutely cannot do either, then accept the fact that the players will develop more slowly than you'd like.

Who Hits With Whom?

In a perfect world, every player would get to hit with a stronger player all the time. But that's not possible. So you generally have players hit with players of roughly the same level. Sometimes you can have a player spend part of a session with a weaker player, and part with a stronger – they balance out. If you can get a practice partner, then if he hits with one of the stronger players, that player can then hit with a weaker player. Some coaches make up hitting partners on the spot. Others keep track (on paper or on a computer) and rotate hitting partners. It's your choice.

Schedule

For a junior class, I've found 4:30-6:30 PM to be a good time, both on weekdays and weekends. Perhaps set up two sessions per week. Don't make the mistake of starting off with too many sessions, and ending up with small numbers in each session. It's better to have a few very good sessions with lots of players than a lot of less successful ones with few players.

General Principles For Coaching Juniors

- Juniors have a shorter attention span. Respect this, and don't expect them to spend large amounts of time continuously on one aspect of the game. It's not that they can't do it – they can – but they won't enjoy it, and they will lose interest in the sport. Instead, vary the practice sessions as much as possible. If there is a specific aspect you want a junior to work extra on, then come back to it, if possible with a different drill that still covers the same technique.

- Juniors have less hand-eye coordination than adults, but a greater learning capacity – they are natural mimics. This means that they can learn specific strokes very well, but they won't have much control over them without much practice. Adults do not learn techniques nearly as well (and you often have to compromise on technique, since they have ingrained bad habits), but they have more ball control. So while an adult may have trouble getting a technique perfect, he'll usually be able to rally better than a junior. A junior will get the technique down perfectly, but will have trouble keeping the ball in play unless the ball comes back the same way every time.

- Treat table tennis as a sport, not a game. This means players must train to improve as well as to have fun. If you run a program where it's all fun and games (i.e. play games, but little table tennis drilling), then the players will treat it like a game – like Parcheesi – and will be quicker to drop it. If you treat it like a sport, the players will respect it, they will work to improve, and they will be more likely to stay with it. On the other hand, don't get too caught up with the idea of trying to make everyone a world-class player. Most are there not only to learn, but to have fun as well. Keep that in mind as you coach.

- Never stress ratings. Ratings have a purpose, but they can terrorize junior players, making them scared to play in tournaments. To many juniors, ratings are like grades, and so they see tournaments the same way they see a test at school. Unfortunately, while you may successfully take a test while nervous, it plays havoc with your table tennis skills. It also takes the fun out of the sport. Stress that improvement is the key, and that their goal should be to play their best. Another option is to stress the idea that ratings are important only when they go up, but irrelevant when they go down. In other words, what is important is not their current rating, but the highest rating achieved – so a player can only "improve" in a tournament, since the highest rating achieved can never go down. Never let juniors feel they are being judged by their ratings.

- Give each player short-, intermediate-, and long-term goals. These goals can be anything from hitting 100 forehands or backhands in a row to winning a specific event at an upcoming tournament. It's always good to give them something to train for – so stress specific upcoming tournaments that they should train for, and attend as a team. You should encourage local tournament directors to hold lower events such as Under 800 or Under 1000 so your younger juniors can play in a competitive event.

- Use simple language to communicate. Younger kids especially do not have large vocabularies, and are hesitant to let you know if they don't understand.

- If at all possible, get team uniforms. It'll help develop team spirit, and greatly increase participation. A junior is never more proud then when wearing his team uniform!

Specific Techniques When Coaching Juniors

Ball Bouncing

Younger kids – 5-10 years old or so – should start out with ball bouncing. This simply means bouncing the ball on their paddle over and over. Younger kids may struggle to do this more than once or twice, due to lower coordination. Ball bouncing is a way to develop the hand-eye coordination needed in table tennis. When they can do this consistently on the forehand side, challenge them to do it on the backhand side, which is trickier. Then have them alternate sides.

Grip

Because they have smaller hands, many juniors tend to put their index finger down the middle of the paddle. This can make the grip too floppy. It's OK for the finger to go down the middle a little bit for younger juniors, but no more than about 45 degrees.

Serves

Juniors have great difficulty in generating spin on their serves. Creating spin involves grazing the ball, which takes a fine touch not yet developed in young juniors. However, they take great delight in whatever spin they do create, so teach them advanced serves early on. Although they usually don't like doing serving practice on their own, they will try out their newly learned serves whenever they play games or in serve & attack drills, and so get practice that way.

Timing

Beginning juniors often have difficulty timing their shots. One way to help them with this is to time it for them – as you rally with them, go "Da-da, da-da,..." timing the "da's" with the ball's contact with the racket and table, so the junior knows when contact should be. You'll be surprised how much this helps beginners, especially juniors.

Drives

When first learning to stroke the ball, it's best to use multi-ball training. A beginning junior simply doesn't have the hand-eye coordination to properly stroke the ball that doesn't come at them perfectly, and they can't keep the ball in play long enough to get a good workout. To keep it fun and interesting, sometimes put a target on the table for them to aim for.

Many juniors tend to point their racket up when stroking forehands or backhands. This is because their elbow is lower than an adult's, and so the table is higher to them. This is okay as long as the racket tip is no more than around 45 degrees upward. Many also tend to stand jammed up to the table, and so are rushed, and have a short, abrupt stroke. Make sure they give themselves time and room for a complete stroke.

Stress consistency. Most juniors want to smash, but they first must learn the proper stroke. Set a reasonable goal of how many they should hit in a row, and keep increasing it until they can hit 100 or so in a row.

Looping
Juniors may have to let the ball drop more when looping than adults. Many coaches (especially from Europe) believe that junior players should start out by learning to loop early on, letting the ball drop down below table level, and topspinning it back. The theory is that it's easier for them to do this, since the ball drops down to a more comfortable level for them, and it allows them to develop topspin control early on. They still start off juniors with regular forehands and backhands, but move to looping as soon as the player has enough control to do so. You may wish to coach this way, or use the standard method of perfecting the forehand and backhand drives first, and then introduce looping.

Pushing
Like serving, juniors often don't have the fine touch needed to create spin yet, and so their pushes are not that spinny. However, especially for younger juniors, the slowness of the push shot allows them to rally longer than with drive shots. It is sometimes important to stress that players should normally play aggressively with topspin. While pushing is important, too much pushing will slow down their development and turn them into passive players, playing to win now (by pushing) rather than developing a more advanced attack.

A Typical Junior Training Schedule

Many junior coaches have found it successful to have sort of an unwritten "contract" with the players. The contract is that if the players work hard the first half, the second half will be mostly games. Serve and attack drills are considered "fun" drills, and can be done at the start of the second half of the session, before going to games.

The drills themselves are usually 15 minutes long, with each player doing 7.5 minutes. (Some drills, such as serve & attack, can be done for ten minutes each.) Stress to the players that both players are drilling at all times. That means that if one player is doing a footwork drill, the other is doing a control drill – practicing ball control and consistency. A typical training session could be divided into the following segments. You should vary the sessions, and when possible tailor the drills to the players. Here's a typical 2-hour session. See Drills Library chapter for examples of drills, or come up with your own.

1. Jogging & Stretching – 5 minutes
2. Forehand & backhand warm-up (drives & loops) – 10 minutes
3. Footwork/Stroking Drill #1 – 15 minutes
4. Footwork/Stroking Drill #2 – 15 minutes
5. Footwork/Stroking Drill #3 – 15 minutes
6. Break – 10 minutes
7. Drill #4 (serve & attack drill) – 20 minutes
8. Games – 30 minutes

Games

It's good to finish off a junior session with some games – let them have fun! There are many options on what to do here. Here are some possibilities:

- **Up-Down Tables.** You start it off by matching the players off against others in no particular order. They play one game, usually to 11. The winners move up a table, and the losers move down a table, and a new series of games begins. If there's an odd number of players, whoever loses on the last table sits out or hits with the coach until the next game finishes.
- **Brazilian Teams.** You start it off by dividing the players into teams of 3-6 each. One player from each team goes to a table and plays a point. The winner stays on the table; the loser goes to the end of the line on his team, and the next player on his team plays the next point. New player always serves. Games can be up to 21, 31, 41 or 51.
- **Doubles.** You can do this up-down table style (see above) or a round robin.
- **Round Robin Tournament.** Put the players in groups so the players in each group are roughly the same level, and play it out.
- **Relay races** are good for younger kids, and is good physical training. They can include regular running, bouncing ball on racket or like a basketball (with paddle), through an obstacle course, etc.
- **Bottle Game.** This is often a favorite for younger kids. You put a bottle of water or a sports drink on the table, and feed multiball. The kids line up and try to hit it, getting two shots each. Tell them the bottle is full of worm juice or something disgusting, and that if they hit it, you have to drink it.

Photo by Mike Yuan

- **Cup Game.** Another favorite of younger kids. Bring a few dozen paper cups, and set them up either bowling fashion (ten at a time) or in pyramids, and you feed each of the kids ten shots and see how many they can knock down. Or have the kids get creative and set up their own pyramids or walls from stacked cups, and then they take turns knocking it down as you feed them multiball (usually two shots each).

Keep It Going!

A junior training program is an ongoing program, with regular meets every week. You may want to have an off season where you close down for a month, but most successful programs run nearly year round. You may break it up into three-month segments, and collect fees for three months at a time, though you should normally allow players to pay per session as well. The key is to reach a critical mass so that there are enough juniors in the program that it becomes their own peer group – and they keep coming back, week after week, month after month, year after year. Most successful junior training programs have a very small turnover. If a 10-year-old plays regularly one year, it's more than likely he will still be there five years later. (It's when they go to college that juniors tend to drop out, but that's a separate issue.)

CHAPTER NINE
Private Coaching

Let's be clear; private coaching is tiring work. If you don't like coaching, it will wear you down until you hate the job. But if you like coaching, and like working with others, it can be an enjoyable activity.

Decide how many hours you want to do private coaching, and what hours you want to do it. During the week, you can get lots of junior students in the afternoon, with more adults at night. On weekends, you can get both. You can also get a number of retired people for daytime coaching.

Do you prefer to coach a lot of hours a few days a week? Or coach nearly every day, but fewer hours? Some coaches find that after coaching for a few years, they can coach nearly every day, almost never taking a day off.

Get a notebook planner of some sort, and write down all scheduled lessons. Staying organized is important. Make sure to have contact information for all students.

What to Charge
Different coaches differ on how much to charge. In a big city, where prices are high, you can charge more. In the country, where prices are lower, you should charge less. I'd recommend charging a minimum of $25/hour, and you may go up to $60/hour or more. Most coaches give discounts to club members and juniors, or non-members simply pay a daily fee in addition to the coaching fee.

Every coach will run into students who arrange a lesson, but don't show. How should you handle this? This is your job, your business, and you can't afford to waste your time. You might let a student get away with it once, but make it clear that if they arrange a time and don't show, they still pay.

What to Teach
How do you go about deciding what to teach in private lessons? Remember the cardinal rule: *The customer is always right!*

What this means is that you coach what the student wants. If a student wants to be an advanced player with advanced technique, that's what you teach him. If a student is aiming for a specific level (especially an older player) or simply wants to work on one part of his game, work with him toward his goals, even if it means not trying to turn him into a world-class player. You'll even find students that just want to hit around or play games. If that's what they want, and they'll pay for it, I suggest you do what they want.

However, most students are going to put it in your hands as to what to do. So what do you do?

If the student isn't a beginner, hit with him for a while, see what he can do, analyze what he needs to do, and then teach him. If he seems unhappy about making changes that you know he needs to do, explain to him that these are long-term techniques that will pay off in the long run. Most students will accept that.

There is a difference between coaching adults and juniors. Adults often have difficulty copying proper technique, and there will be times where you'll want to pull your hair out when a player seems to stubbornly do a stroke the wrong way no matter how hard you try to fix the problem. Juniors tend to pick up new and proper techniques much more easily – they are more natural mimics. On the other hand, adults have more natural ball control, and so can rally longer. They also have more patience, and so can work longer on a specific technique.

Break down each one-hour lesson into several segments. Start with a warm-up. Then work on basic shots. Then get to more advanced shots. Perhaps finish with serve and receive. If you are doing multi-ball, and there are balls all over, go to ball pick-up a few minutes before the lesson ends so you'll be on time for the next student. (Make sure the student helps pick up balls!)

Try to set up a regular lineup on your coaching days. It's not very convenient for you if you coach an hour, have an hour off, coach an hour, have an hour off, etc. For example, you might have a 6-9PM lineup on Wednesdays; if your 7PM student stops taking lessons, then actively promote that spot.

CHAPTER TEN
Keeping Players Interested

Many coaches lose students as fast as they get them. Why? Because they don't really understand what the student wants. And students run the whole range from those who just want to have fun to those who are very serious about improving. You need to learn to tell just what the student wants, and give it to him. Remember – the student is always right! (At least in this respect.)

Carlos Ko stayed interested long enough to learn to do this. So can your students. Photo by John Oros

However, some aspects are constant. You need to keep it fun. A coach who is obviously unhappy with his work or so serious he never smiles isn't going to inspire students. You need to find a balance. You may put your student through lots of drills, but every now and then break things up. Lob a few balls (or let the student lob), crack a few jokes, have fun.

At the same time, you must treat the sport as just that – a sport. The only thing worse than a coach who is too serious is one who treats the sport like a game. Some coaches are always preaching how fun is all that matters, and they mostly let the players play games or other fun activities, but don't really train them. The players aren't required to put in an investment in the sport, and so don't take it seriously as a sport. They might as well be playing Parcheesi.

So you must find a balance between seriousness and fun. Treat it like the Olympic sport it is, but have fun as you do so.

For a junior class, you should stress the team aspect as much as possible. The quickest way to turn a semi-serious junior player into a more serious one who comes back over and over is to get team uniforms. Kids like to be part of a team, and if they have team uniforms, they get that much more enjoyment out of it, and that much more incentive to come back.

More than anything else, remember that the players in a group session, whether adults or juniors, are their own peer group. If a ten-week class comes to an end, make sure the group gets back together, perhaps at the same time and day as the class. The juniors in your junior class are their peer group, which is why it's so important to have a large enough group so it's diverse enough so they all feel like they are a part of a team.

Table tennis is like a drug. Get them addicted, and they'll keep coming back for more. You're the supplier. Go to it!

CHAPTER ELEVEN
Drills Library

Jogging and Stretching
You should start off all sessions with some easy jogging to loosen the muscles, and then a stretching routine. Since you often don't know who will show up for the specific class in advance, this is a good time to work out who hits with whom. For this reason, it's a good idea to have one of the juniors lead in stretching while you make plans.

Basics Drills
Beginning players especially need to work on the basics. So don't forget to have them practice standard forehand to forehand, backhand to backhand (and don't forget down the lines!), pushing drills, etc. More advanced players mostly do this as part of their warm-up.

Forehand & Backhand Drive and Loop Warm-up
To start off a session, have the players hit forehand-to-forehand and backhand-to-backhand, as a warm-up, for five to ten minutes each. Advanced players will switch to looping after five minutes or so. Players may also combine these warm-up drills with footwork drills.

Footwork/Stroking Drills
Here are some footwork drills. Players can hit or loop these shots, depending on their style and level, and feel free to come up with your own variations. One common variation: after 3-5 repetitions of a drill sequence, it becomes free play. Another is to start the drill with a loop against backspin, or to start the drill with serve and receive. Generally each player does the drill for about 7.5 minutes each.

A. **One-one footwork:** Player A moves side to side, hitting all forehands to Player B's backhand (or forehand), who hits the ball side to side. Drill normally covers about 2/3 of the table, either the forehand or backhand side. Faster players can cover entire table.

B. **Forehand-backhand footwork:** Player A alternates forehand and backhand shots to Player B's backhand (or forehand). B hits side to side to wide corners.

C. **Falkenberg drill**: Player A hits everything into B's backhand. The three-shot sequence for Player A is backhand from backhand side;

forehand from backhand side; forehand from forehand side. (The drill is named after the Falkenberg club in Sweden, where 1971 World Champion Stellan Bengtsson popularized the drill.)

D. **Random footwork:** Player A hits balls with forehand or backhand to Player B's backhand. (You can also do this to the forehand.) Player B hits balls randomly either to Player A's forehand or backhand, so Player A has to be ready for both. When Player A is proficient at this, then Player B should put the ball anywhere, including to the middle (the playing elbow).

E. **Forehand (or Backhand) random footwork**: Player B hit to half to two-thirds of Player A's forehand side, and Player A plays all forehand. Or B hits balls to A's backhand side, and A plays all backhand.

F. Player A loops two forehands crosscourt to Player B's forehand, who blocks. B blocks second loop to A's middle, who loops another forehand to B's forehand. B blocks that ball down line to A's backhand, and A loops forehand from backhand side, crosscourt to B's backhand. B blocks down the line to A's forehand, and we start over again. Alternate version: A's loop from the middle goes to B's backhand, who blocks crosscourt to A's backhand, and the drill continues as above.

G. Player A plays everything into Player B's backhand. The four-shot sequence is as follows: A hits backhand from backhand; A loops forehand from middle; A hits backhand from backhand; A loops forehand down line from forehand. At advanced levels, the shots to A's middle and backhand can be random, so A has to be ready to cover either the middle or forehand with his forehand.

H. Player A loops two balls from forehand side down the line to B's backhand. B blocks second one crosscourt to A's backhand. A hits backhand down line to B's forehand. And then we repeat, except now the two players switch rolls with B looping two forehands down line to A's backhand, A blocks crosscourt, etc. So in this drill, both players get to attack and block. Since both players are doing the drill, the drill is done in about 7.5 minutes.

I.   Player A serves short backspin. B pushes to A's backhand. A backhand loops down line to B's forehand. B blocks crosscourt to A's forehand. A forehand loops crosscourt. B blocks to middle, and then it's free play.

J.   Any of the infinite number of drills you can come up with. Or ask top players and coaches about their favorite drills.

Serve & Attack Drills

There are two main ways of doing this drill. One way is for the server to serve backspin, the receiver pushes it back to a pre-arranged spot or area, and the server attacks, usually with a loop. The other way is for the server to serve anything, the receiver returns as if it were a game (or perhaps playing slightly more control so server can attack), and server attacks. You can vary this latter by sometimes restricting the receive. For example, if the server serves short to the forehand, the receiver may have the option of flipping crosscourt or dropping the ball short, i.e. can't flip down the line. Generally each player does the drill 7.5 to 10 minutes each.

There are a huge number possible ways to do this drill. For example, Player A serves short backspin to forehand. Player B pushes quick to A's backhand. A backhand loops down the line to B's forehand. Then both counterloop and free play.

Or Player A serves short backspin to the middle. Player B pushes deep to the corner. A loops (forehand or backhand) to B's backhand. B blocks to A's forehand. A loops to B's middle, and then it's free play.

Other variations include the receiver flipping the serve (which doesn't have to always be backspin), or dropping it short, or any other variation you can think of. For beginning/intermediate players, keep it relatively simple, with the first few shots known, then free play. As they advance, intermediate/advanced players can incorporate more randomness and complexity into their drills.

Note that serve and attack drills are where players can practice their serves, although players should be encouraged to practice serves on their own. (Another option is to devote part of the practice session to serve practice alone, or do so right after the session.)

CHAPTER TWELVE
Sample Flyers

On the next two pages are sample flyers for a **Beginning Class** and for a **Junior Training Program**. (They are shrunk down a bit since the originals were on 8.5x11 pages.) Below is a sample press release to send to a newspaper's Calendar Section. (See chapter on Recruiting Students for more info on this.)

To:	Calendar Section, Washington Post
From:	Larry Hodges, Maryland Table Tennis Center
Subject:	Junior Table Tennis Training
Date:	January 1, 2010

Would it be possible to include the following in your Calendar Section? The Maryland Table Tennis Center in Gaithersburg, Md., has junior training sessions on Thursdays, Saturdays and Sundays, 4:30-6:30 PM, for players aged 7 to 17. Coaching the sessions will be USATT Certified National Coach Larry Hodges. The training will cover the basics of table tennis, including basic strokes, serve and return of serve, tactics, footwork and equipment. Fee is $150 for 20 sessions. For more information, contact Coach Hodges at 301-519-8580 or larry@larrytt.com. Thank you.

Beginning Table Tennis Class
at the
Maryland Table Tennis Center
18761-Q Frederick Rd., Gaithersburg, MD 20879 • 301-519-8580 • www.mdttc.com

Dates: 10 Mondays, April 2 – June 4, 2001

Times: 7:00 – 8:30 PM

Fees: $100/student. Make checks out to Maryland Table Tennis Center. Join USATT for an additional $30/year ($20 if under age 18), and get 6 copies of their glossy bi-monthly magazine as well as information on tournaments, clubs and other info. It also allows you to join the USATT Rating System.

Coach: Larry Hodges, USATT Certified Coach. See www.larrytt.com. Assistant coaches may be hired, depending on turnout.

Items Covered: The goal of the class is to teach the basics of table tennis. Techniques to be taught include the basic strokes, serve and return of serve, tactics, footwork and equipment.

Directions: From the Beltway (495), take 270 North. Go to exit 11, Montgomery Village Ave. Drive 1/4 mile to first traffic light, Frederick Rd. (355), and turn left. Drive 1.1 miles and turn right at Econo Lodge sign (steep uphill). Go 100 yards until road dead ends, and turn left. Go 100 yards and take first left-hand turn into MDTTC parking lot.

More Info: Contact Larry Hodges, 301-519-8580, larry@larrytt.com

---

Participant's Name_____ Date of Birth_____

Address_____

Home Phone_____ Work Phone_____ Email_____

I accept full responsibility for my participation. I relieve the coaches, directors, sponsors and any others involved in the class of any liability for injury, loss or damages.

Signature_____ Date_____

Junior Table Tennis Training

at the

Maryland Table Tennis Center

18761-Q Frederick Rd., Gaithersburg, MD 20879 • 301-519-8580 • www.mdttc.com

Times: Thursdays, Saturdays & Sundays, 4:30-6:30 PM

Ages/Levels: Ages 7-17, all levels

Fees: $200/20 sessions. Make checks out to Maryland Table Tennis Center

Coaches: USATT Certified Coaches Cheng Yinghua, Jack Huang, Larry Hodges
                    (usually two coaches/session)

Info: Contact Larry Hodges, 301-519-8580, larry@larrytt.com

Directions: From the Beltway (495), take 270 North. Go to exit 11, Montgomery
                    Village Ave. Drive 1/4 mile to first traffic light, Frederick Rd. (355), and
                    turn left. Drive 1.1 miles and turn right at Econo Lodge sign (steep uphill).
                    Go 100 yards until road dead ends, and turn left. Go 100 yards and take
                    first left-hand turn into MDTTC parking lot.

Participant's Name_____ Date of Birth_____

Address_____

Home Phone_____ Work Phone_____ Email_____

I accept full responsibility for my and my children's participation. I relieve the coaches,
directors, sponsors and any others involved in the class of any liability for injury, loss or
damages.

Signature_____ Date_____
(Parents sign for those under 18)

CHAPTER THIRTEEN
Helpful Links & Resources

Links
- USA Table Tennis, www.usatt.org
- USATT Coaching,
  http://www.teamusa.org/USA-Table-Tennis/Coaching.aspx
- International Table Tennis Federation, www.ittf.com
- National Collegiate Table Tennis Association, www.nctta.org
- Paralympic Table Tennis,
  http://www.teamusa.org/USA-Table-Tennis/Para-News.aspx
- Laws of Table Tennis,
  www.ittf.com/ITTF_Hand_Book/2_Handbook.pdf
- USOC Ethics of Coaching (or search for "USA Olympic Coaching Ethics Code")
  http://assets.teamusa.org/assets/documents/attached_file/filename/1906/USOCCoachingEthicsCode.pdf

Books
- Table Tennis Tactics for Thinkers, by Larry Hodges (2013)
- ITTF's Level 1 Coaching Manual, by Glen Tepper (2003)
- ITTF's Advanced Coaching Manual, by Philippe Molodzoff (2008)
- Table Tennis: Steps to Success, by Richard McAfee (2009)
- Table Tennis: Steps to Success, by Larry Hodges (1993, updated 2007) (Yes, there are two versions with the same title.)
- Table Tennis Tales & Techniques, by Larry Hodges (2009)
- Train to Win, by Michel Gadal (1997)
- Winning Table Tennis, by Dan Seemiller and Mark Holowchak (1996)

Videos
- *Modern Table Tennis 101* and *102* by Sean O'Neill and Wei Wang
- *Complete Table Tennis* by Dan Seemiller and Mark Nordby
- *Textbook Table Tennis* by Brian Pace
- *Killerspin Success in Table Tennis* by Killerspin
- *Table Tennis the Sport* by Scott Preiss
- *Pro Table Tennis Serves* by Alpha Productions
- *Pro Table Tennis Strokes* by Alpha Productions

About the Author

Larry Hodges (larry@larrytt.com), a member of the USATT Hall of Fame and a long-time coach at the Maryland Table Tennis Center, is certified by USA Table Tennis as a National Coach. He is the Author of *Table Tennis Tactics for Thinkers, Table Tennis: Steps to Success, Table Tennis Tales & Techniques*, and *Instructor's Guide to Table Tennis*, and over 600 coaching articles. He was editor of *USA Table Tennis Magazine* for twelve years, chaired the USATT Coaching Committee from 1991-95, and was USATT's 2002 Developmental Coach of the Year.

39029429R00027

Made in the USA
Lexington, KY
07 February 2015